Crochet for Beginners

A Complete Guide with Illustrations to Learn Crocheting and Create Your Favorite Patterns in Complete Autonomy

By

Kayla Jayne

responsibility or blame be held against the publisher for any reparation, damages, or monetary loss due to the information herein, either directly or indirectly.

Respective authors own all copyrights not held by the publisher.

The information herein is offered for informational purposes solely, and is universal as so. The presentation of the information is without contract or any type of guarantee assurance.

The trademarks that are used are without any consent, and the publication of the trademark is without permission or backing by the trademark owner. All trademarks and brands within this book are for clarifying purposes only and are the owned by the owners themselves, not affiliated with this document.

Table of Contents

Introduction

Crochet differs from weaving in that stitches are made with a one hook instead of a pair of needles, and the fabric is not 'cast-off' on the end. Most of the time, the finished result is thicker than the material woven from the same yarn; after you have gained experience and confidence, the work 'starts to grow' much more quickly than crochet does.

Crochet is a pleasurable and fantastic activity in which you may knit your own garments, develop your own designs, and use them. It is also, without a doubt, an amazing method to use your talent to generate income. It goes without saying that if you are just getting started with crochet, a good beginners' guide to crochet will be of tremendous assistance.

The first element that will come to mind is likely to be the materials that you will want in order to begin your crochet learning journey. Crochet needles and yarn are two of the most important items you'll need for your project. You may knit using a variety of yarn sizes and types and shapes of needles. Crochet is a versatile art form that can be practised by everyone. If you purchase a more comprehensive beginner's crochet handbook, you would be able to identify them one by one and in detail, generally, you must be aware that crochet needles will be presented in various quantities. For your first task, the needles numbered 7 & 8 will become the typical sizes, with the possibility of a choose size as well. Keep in mind that the more the amount, the bigger your fine needles will be, and the looser the knits will be. However, the choice of the needle is mostly determined by the nature of the work.

The book will teach you how easy it is to put aside some "you" time with only a hook or some yarn. In just a few short weeks, you would be delving into your creative side via easy step-by-step health exercises and gorgeously inspired crochet designs. You will also learn how to employ the relaxing rhythmic practice of crochet to encourage a more thoughtful way of living.

Being the crocheter, you are well aware of the fact that it is therapeutic. You may, on the other hand, learn to optimize those advantages and use crocheting to consciously increase your overall well-being. Having this understanding will assist you in weathering life's unavoidable storms and continuing to live effectively despite these circumstances.

I have to admit that I am not very good at crocheting! Fortunately, you don't have to be an experienced to benefit from crochet therapy; thus, whether you're a novice or a professional, a little crochet therapy may do wonders for your mental health. Enjoy a visualization exercise that requires you on a stroll along the seashore, some mindful memories to represent on, motivation, relaxation, or even a little daydreaming during the process.

It was a life-changing event for me when I first started learning how to crochet and knit. The patterns in this guide are based on the information I have gathered over the decades as a well-being coach, clinician, and researcher, but they are also founded on my years of experience as a designer and maker.

Chapter 1: Crochet Basics

Crochet is a needlework technique that includes creating a piece using a crochet hook and fibre or another similar material. It is most typically crochet thread or yarn, but it might also be wire, cloth, twine, or any other kind of material.

Crochet lovers are motivated to complete crochet items that are typically practical, visually beautiful, or beneficial in some way. Afghans, baby booties, baby blankets, tote bags, scarves, granny squares, shawls, purses, hats, and other popular goods are all made from crochet. A variety of objects, including socks, jewellery, and curtains, may be made using the crochet technique.

It is also possible to crochet a range of components to be used in other projects in addition to garments. Crafting crocheted or knitted trimmings and edgings is a common chore that may be applied to a variety of products, including crocheted, knitted, and sewn goods (including ready-made items.) You might, for example, buy some socks, towels, and pillows and crochet an edging on each of them to give them a personal touch.

1.1 Origin of crocheting

Historically, crochet has been regarded as a valuable textile processing method, and it has been used for historical objects since the 1800s. Crochet, or crocheting, is an art form that includes creating patterns using a crochet hook and a matching yarn in order to create a variety of structures and shapes by employing a variety of stitches and methods. Crocheting was initially employed primarily for the purpose of making nets.

As opposed to crochet, crocheting makes use of a single crochet hook rather than two pointed needles, which seems to be the case with crochet. The name "needle" is misleading since, unlike crochet needles, this one has a hook at the end, which is why the word "needle" may be misleading. Crochet hooks are used to take up the yarn and to create the stitches in crochet patterns.

Crochet can produce stitches that are far tighter and stronger than crochet, which is why crocheted clothing is frequently harder and studier in appearance. Crocheted patterns that are softer and less solid, on the other hand, may be created by utilizing the right stitches. Of course, there are other factors to consider as well, such as the stitches utilized, the kind of yarn used, the size of the crochet hook used, and your own personal crocheting skill (firm or loose).

In addition, solid crochet stitches that retain their shape make it simple to create three-dimensional items such as Amigurumi (small and large crocheted figures), baskets, and other household products.

1.2 Basic crochet supplies

The essential tools you'll need to get started are a crochet hook and thread, yarn, or wire to make your material.

- **Crochet hooks** — Available in various gauges depending on the thickness of the material to be looped, these metal or plastic tools come in various sizes.

- **Yarn and crochet threads** – Choosing your fibers is one of the most appealing parts of crocheting. Again, the kind of yarn or thread you'll need will be determined by what you're making.

- **Scissors** – Some of the favorite craft scissors are made by Fiskars.

- **Stitch markers** – These little locket-shaped parts will help you stay on track with your designs.

There are many different crochet stitches, but most crafts need to know how to form a slip knot to get the yarn on the hook and the chain stitch to make a solid row to anchor the whole work.

1.3 Crochet types

Alternatively, to embroidery and quilting, crochet is available in a range of styles to choose from. There is a vast variety of potential consequences for these styles, which were developed in numerous places according to local customs. These methods highlight the versatility of Crochet as an art form, whether they are used to create delicate lace or massive woven baskets of different sizes. Here are a few strategies you may want to think about using, depending on the final outcome you want to achieve.

- **Aran:** Aran is a textured yarn that is often used for bulky sweaters and blankets. It's a Celtic technique that involves several interwoven crochet cables and is also termed cable crochet. Aran is also named for moderately weight yarn that is more frequently known in the United States as worsted yarn. Don't be confused: Aran crochet does not need the usage of Aran yarn.

- **Bavarian:** Bavarian Crochet is the intermediate method that is often used to construct blankets and shawls. It is typically done in rounds rather than rows. The end product is a thick cloth with delicate color gradations.

- **Jiffy lace:** This traditional 19th-century method is also known as broomstick lace. A hook and a long wooden dowel are used. "The pattern is formed by pulling long loops of the thread up onto the dowel (traditionally, a broomstick, that is where the term derives from)," according to Red Heart.

- **Bosnian:** Frequently mistaken for crochet, Bosnian Crochet, usually called Shepherd's crochet, is made entirely of the slip stitch. While a conventional crochet hook may be used, some people prefer to use Bosnian crochet hooks since they are simpler to work with. Because the procedure is time-consuming, it is best used to make smaller items.

- **Cro-Hook:** A cro-hook is a double-sided hook used in this Tunisian crochet style. This lets you produce double-sided cloth by working in two colors at the same time. Cro-knit, double-ended Tunisian, and double hook crochet are all terms for the same method, ideal for making multi-colored scarves and blankets.

- **Clothesline:** This African and Nepalese method includes utilizing thick rope or chain to produce a strong, durable fabric often used to make baskets, bags, and carpets.

- **Irish lace:** This method, also known as Irish lace, requires using extremely fine crochet hooks and linen or cotton thread. Its usage dates back to the nineteenth century when the Irish created it to replicate more costly Venetian lace. After the Irish Potato Famine, the skill was utilized to boost the economy, and by the mid-nineteenth century, about 12,000 Irish women were crocheting.

- **Tunisian:** Tunisian Crochet is a common method that involves using a crochet hook that is exceptionally long and has a stopper at the end. It's also known as Afghan crochet, and it's similar to crochet as it involves working numerous loops at once. The method creates a noticeably thick fabric and less malleable fabric than other crochet styles, making it ideal for blankets and winter caps rather than the softer wearable goods.

- **Tapestry:** A beautiful method for making colorful and patterned textiles, tapestry crochet employs a variety of colored yarns to create a fabric that seems nearly woven rather than crocheted. Similar methods are known as intarsia, colorwork, jacquard, and mosaic Crochet. Tapestry crochet is widely used by the native Wayuu people of Venezuela and Colombia to construct little purses known as mochila. In Guatemala and Africa, it is used to produce hats.

- **Amigurumi:** This Japanese crochet technique is used to make little stuffed yarn animals. They're very popular because of their adorable look, and they're usually made using simple crochet stitches. To achieve a tight weave, smaller gauge crochet hooks are used.

1.4 Tips for beginners

Learning a new skill is never an easy process. In case you've made the decision that it's finally time to learn to crochet, you've come to the ideal site. These books provide you with everything you'll need to get started (hooks, patterns, yarn, and tips from the experts). Here are some recommendations for crocheting for complete beginners:

1. Keep your stitches flexible and relaxed.

When you're learning anything new, it's normal to feel nervous. The more intricate the Stitch, the more tightly you will grasp your hook. Refrain from doing so, take a deep breath, and keep the stitches slack and relaxed. The looser the stitches are, the simpler it will be to enter your hook and complete the project!

2. Practice.

Before you begin, read over the pattern you want to create. If you notice a stitch you've never attempted before (like single Crochet, shell stitches, double Crochet), take your hook and yarn and practice them before beginning your project. By the time you get to that Stitch in the design, you'll be completely confident in your ability to execute it.

Most designs call for a "gauge swatch," which is often a square sample measuring 4" x 4". While producing the gauge swatch, practice your new stitches to improve your technique and ensure that you are crocheting the product to the right size.

3. Experiment using various tools.

If you're new to start crocheting, it's a good idea to buy a couple of different hooks to experiment with. You could need a hook with the deeper bowl/ mouth if you're having trouble catching the loop on your hook. If you're having trouble placing your hook into the Stitch, you may need a hook with the pointier head. A new hook might be the difference between success and failure.

4. Experiment with various yarns.

Beginners should choose worsted weight yarn that is smooth and doesn't split easily (Brava Worsted is recommended). However, everyone has their preferences. Feel free to experiment with various yarns.

5. Understand the concept of gauge.

This is a frequent beginner error to avoid. It's all about the Gauge! Gauge is a measurement that informs you how many rows and stitches your crochet pattern should fit into a certain number of inches. This should be included in every pattern. If you want your completed creation to look like the photographs or fit in a certain size, you'll need to match your gauge to the pattern's specifications. Many people miss this stage and wind up with a big enough hat as a chair cover. Try to learn about gauge early; it'll pay later!

6. To frog or not to frog, that is the question!

What exactly is frogging? It's when you "rip it." If you pay close attention to detail and notice a mistake the few rows back, it's worth frogging back and correcting the error (it will bug you forever). If the error isn't obvious, consider if you want to go back and correct it. Everybody has different choices. Don't feel bad about your decision.

7. Don't put too much pressure on yourself.

Mistakes are bound to occur. Even the most skilled and meticulous crocheters make errors from time to time. There is no such thing as a flawless first project (first 10 projects). Don't be too hard on yourself if you make a mistake. Be proud of what you've learned, and know that you'll become better with practice.

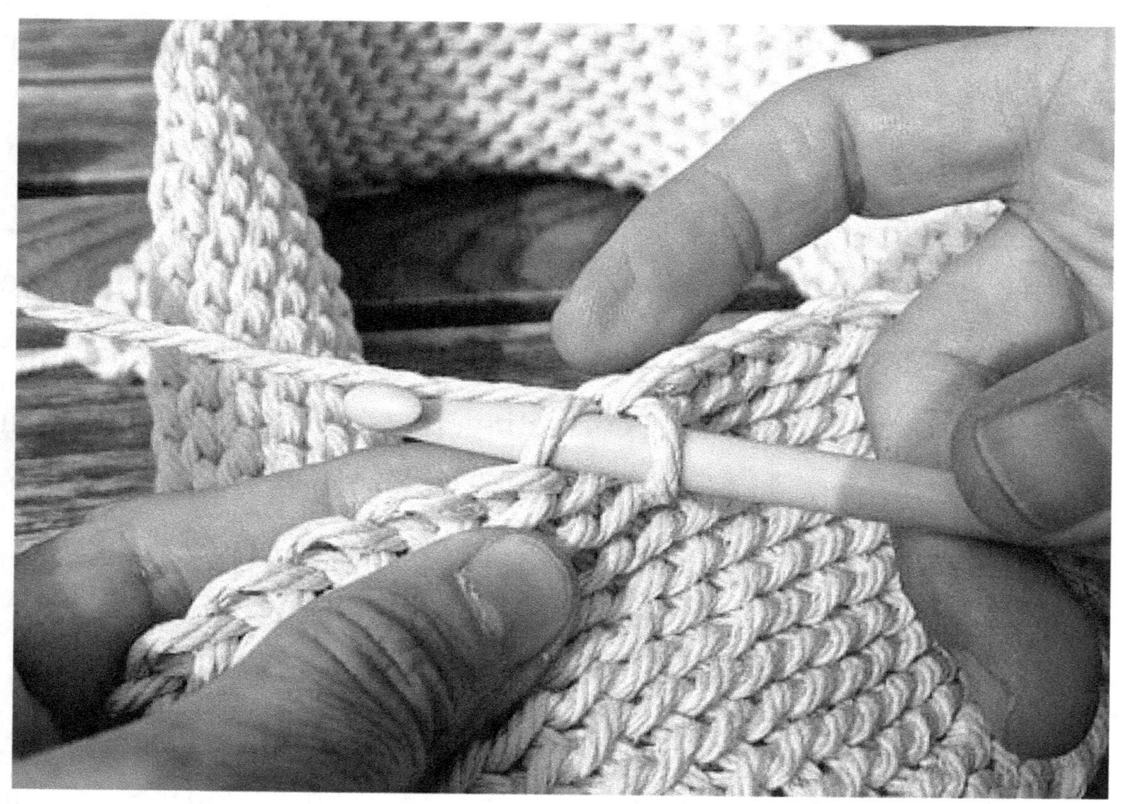

Chapter 2: Crochet Techniques

This section starts with the fundamentals of crochet techniques. If you are a newbie, some of the illustrated instructions are a great place to start with.

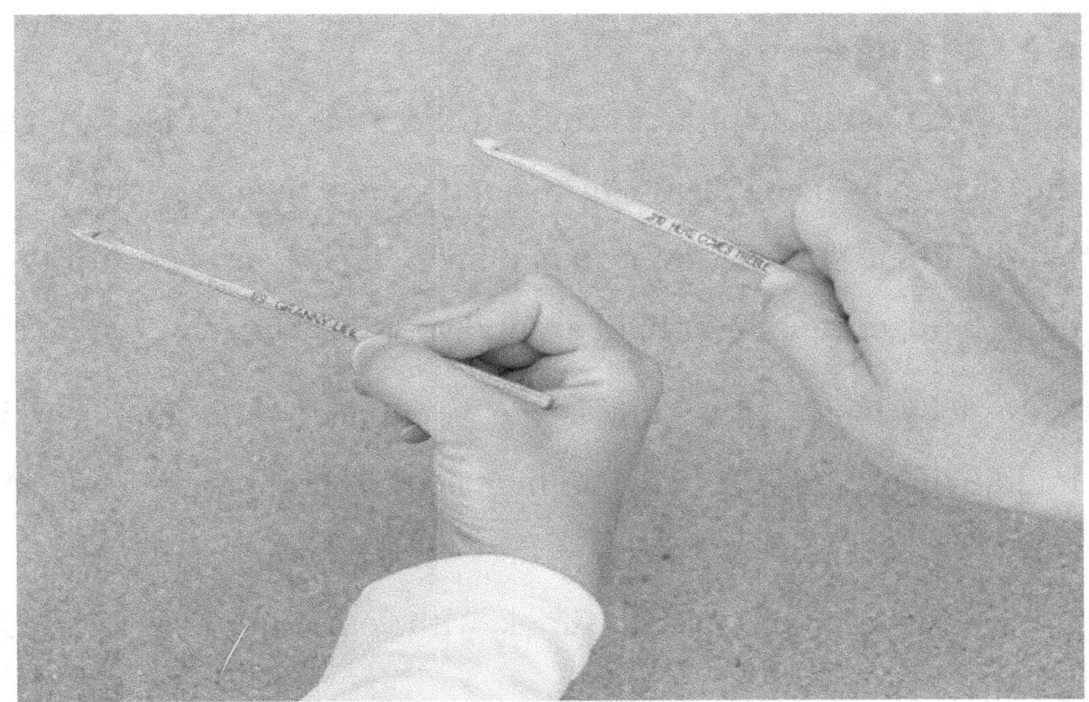

2.1 Holding a hook

- **Pen Position:** Just like you pick up a pencil or pen, pick up your hook. Then twist your hand while a palm is pointing upward, whereas the hook is stabilized in hand and laying in the gap among your thumb and index finger while holding the hook loosely between your fingers and thumb.

- **Knife Position:** You can switch to a knife position if you work with a big hook and thick yarn. Being overly tensed might harm your shoulder or arm while crocheting. Make sure you constantly take breaks and are comfortable.

2.2 Holding a yarn

With your palm facing upwards and the short end in front, Pick the yarn up by using the opposite hand's small finger. Rotate your hand so that the yarn over your pointer finger and beneath the other 2 fingers and tight right around your little finger.

Keep your hand with palm facing your face, your thumb and middle finger poised to take up the task. Using the same hand, A slip knot between your center finger and thumb, right under a crochet hook & loops over the hook, with your index finger curled slightly.

2.3 Holding your yarn, hook, and crochet

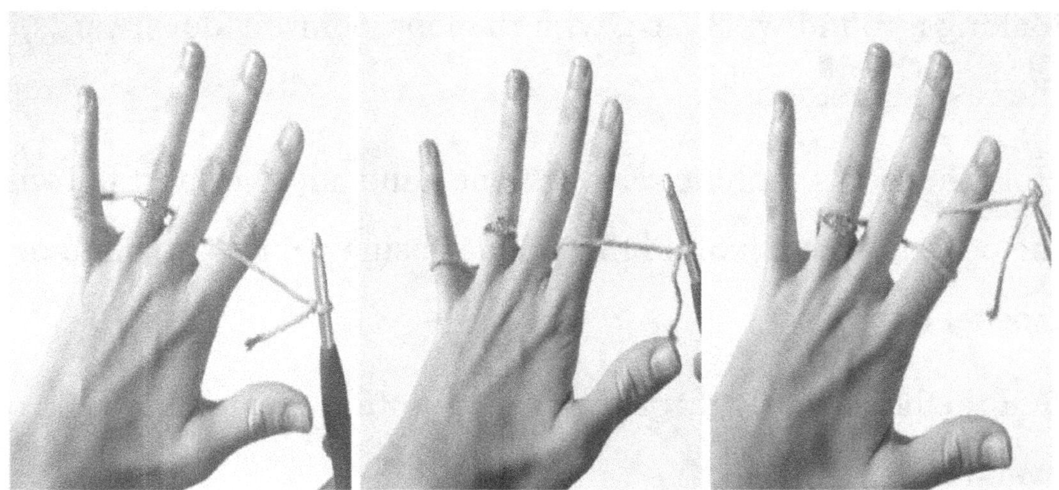

Hold the slip knot between your middle thumb and middle finger, below the crochet hook, and the loop/s with the hook with the same hand.

To maintain the loop slack, loosen a yarn on your index finger. If you stretch your index finger, the yarn will become too tight to drag through the loop on the hook. Many left-handed persons learn to crochet using the hook in their left hand and the yarn in their right hand.

Hold the yarn from below with an upward-pointing hook. Turn the hook so the loop faces downward, and gently draw the yarn out through the continuous loop on a hook. A hook's loop should be kept loose enough for the hook to go through.

Making the slip knot

Making a round with yarn, with the loop pointing downwards, is the easiest method.

Hold the loop's center circle with one hand and the short tail with the other. Make a loop in the circular using your spare hand or a crochet hook.

Pull the hook gently through the loop until it creates a loose loop over a hook.

2.4 How to begin to crochet Stitch?

The process of a loop being dragged through another loop with a hook is the basis of all crochet stitches. Right-handed crocheters work from right to left.

Start using 8ply yarn & 3.50mm sized hook / 4ply yarn & 2.50mm sized hook while learning the basics, so all stitches are visible. Before trying finer threads, learn the basic processes first. Unless otherwise specified, pick up 2 top threads of each Stitch while crocheting. The front and rear loops make up the two upper threads. Follow the following steps:

Step 1.

For loop making:

- Hold the thread at the end with the left hand's thumb and forefinger.

- Make a loop with your right hand by looping the long thread over a small thread.

- Place this loop between your thumb and fingers on your left hand.

Step 2.

- Grasp the wide bar of the hook with your right hand as if it were a pencil.

- Slip the hook under a long thread and through the loop. Grasp the long end of the thread with your right hand. Draw the loop all the way through.

- Don't pull the hook out of the thread.

Step 3.

- Pull the short end of the thread and ball thread in different directions to tighten the loop around the hook's end.

2.5 What to do with the left hand?

Step 4.

- Measure around 10cm down the ball thread from a loop on a hook using your eye.

- With the palm of a hand facing up, place the thread between the ring and little fingers around this place.

Step 5.

- Take the thread behind your hand, under your little and ring fingers, across your middle finger, and under your forefinger to the thumb.

Step 6.

- Hold the hook and loop with the left hand's thumb and fingers.

- Gently draw the ball thread over the fingers so that it is snug but not too tight.

- Grasp the loop's knot between thumb and fingers.

2.6 What to do with the right hand

Step 7.

- Take a pencil-like grip on the wide bar of the hook.

- Bring your middle finger forward and lay it at the hook's tip.

Step 8.

- · Adjust the left hand's fingers: the middle finger is bent to manage tension, while the ring and little fingers control the thread. The hook should move freely and evenly in the right hand, while the thread should move freely and evenly in the left. With time and experience, you'll be able to do it with ease.

2.7 Chain (ch) Crocheting

All crocheting is built on this basis. Chain is used to start crocheting, provide height at the start of a row, and design designs that need an opening or hole. Work the chain stitches looser than the subsequent rows while crocheting the first row (foundation chain).

Step 9.

- Thread the hook through the thread and grab it with the hook. The technique is known as "thread over" or "yarn over hook."

- Pull the thread through a hook's loop. This results in a single chain (ch). A stitch does not include the loop on a hook.

Step 10.

- Rep Step 9 until you get the desired number of chains (ch) - one loop should always remain on the hook.

- Keep the thumb and forefinger of your left hand near a stitch you're working on.

- Practice chain stitches until they're all the same size.

2.8 Slip Stitch (sl st)

In circular crocheting, slip stitching has been used to move across a row without producing depth and join rounds.

Thread the hook through a stitch and loop on the hook in one movement by inserting it from the front, beneath the two top threads of the Stitch adjacent to the hook, threading over and drawing it through both the Stitch and the loop on the hook.

2.9 Half Treble (htr)

Create a chain length, thread it over, and hook it under the 2 top threads of the third ch from the hook, inserting from the front. Draw the thread across and through this ch. Thread over and pull it through all three loops on the hook; one loop will stay on the hook. Completed one-half treble (1htr). Thread over, put a hook under the 2 top threads of the next ch, and continue as before for the next htr.

2.10 Double Crochet (dc)

Make a chain length and hook it under two top threads of the second chain from a hook from the front. Turn the thread over.

Pass it through the chain; the hook now has two loops. Turn the thread over. One loop will stay on the hook after drawing through the two loops. Now you've finished one double Crochet (dc). Insert the hook beneath the two top threads of the next Stitch & repeat as necessary for the next dc.

2.11 Treble (tr)

Make a chain length, thread it over, and insert a hook from the front, beneath the two top threads of the fourth ch from the hook.

Draw the thread through this ch. Thread across all three loops on the hook. Draw it through two loops, leaving two loops on the hook, then thread it over. Draw it through the last two loops, leaving one on the hook.

One treble (1tr) is finished. Thread over, put a hook under the 2 top threads of a next ch, and repeat as necessary for the next tr.

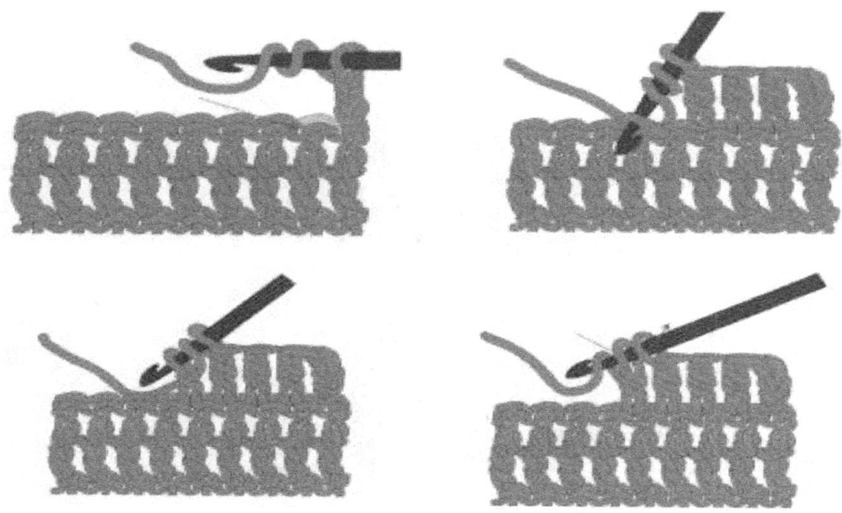

2.12 Double Treble (dtr)

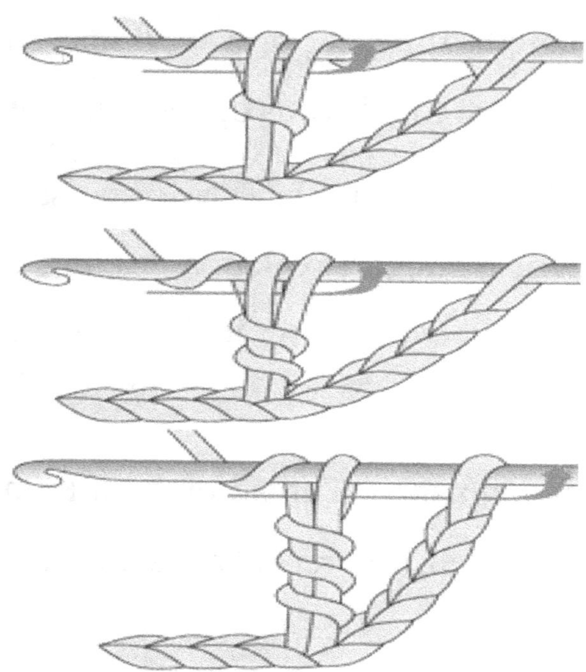

Make a chain length, thread it over twice, put a hook from the front, under the 2 top threads of a 5th ch from a hook, thread over, and pull it through the ch. There are now 4 loops on the hook; thread over and draw it through 2 loops; 3 loops will remain on the hook; thread over and draw it through 2 loops; 2 loops will remain on the hook; thread over again and draw it through the remaining 2 loops; 1 loop will remain on the hook; thread over and draw it through the remaining 2 loops; 1 loop will remain on the hook. One double treble (1dtr) has now been completed.

Thread a hook under the 2 top threads of a next ch and continue as before for the next dtr.

2.13 Triple Treble (triptr)

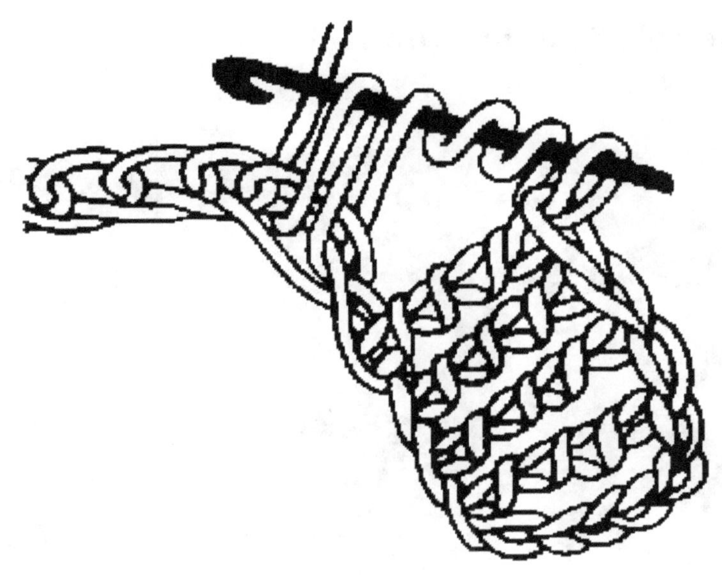

Make a chain length, thread it three times, enter the hook from the front, under the 2 top threads of a 6th ch from a hook, thread it over, and pull it through the ch. There are now 5 loops on the hook; thread over and draw it through 2 loops; 4 loops will remain on the hook; thread over and draw it through 2 loops; 3 loops will remain on the hook; thread over again and draw it through 2 loops; 2 loops will remain on the hook; thread over and draw it through the remaining 2 loops; 1 loop will remain on the hook; thread over again and draw it through the remaining 2 loops; 1 loop will remain on the hook; thread over and draw it through, and the first triple treble (triptr) has finally been achieved.

Thread over three times, place the hook beneath the two top threads of a next ch and continue as before for the following triptr.

2.14 Quadruple Treble (quadtr)

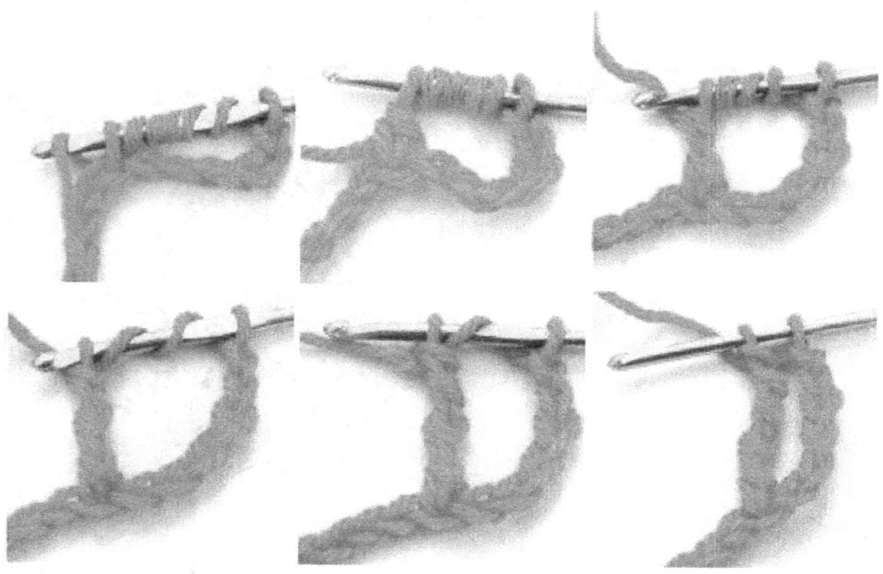

Make a chain length, thread it over four times, then put a hook from the front, under the 2 top threads of a 7th ch from a hook, thread over, and pull it through the ch. There are now 6 loops on the hook; thread over and draw it through 2 loops; 5 loops will remain on the hook; thread over and draw it through 2 loops; 4 loops will remain on the hook; thread over and draw it through 2 loops; 3 loops will remain on the hook; thread over again and draw it through 2 loops; 2 loops will remain on the hook; thread over and draw it through the remaining 2 loops; 1 loop will remain on the hook; thread over again and draw it through and the first quadruple treble (1quadtr) is now finished.

Thread over four times for the next quarter, then put the hook beneath the 2 top threads of a next ch and continue as previously.

2.15 Quintuple Treble (quintr)

Make a chain length, thread it five times, then put the hook from the front, under the 2 top threads of an eighth ch from a hook, thread over, and pull it through a ch. There are now 7 loops on the hook; thread over and draw it through 2 loops; 6 loops will remain on the hook; thread over and draw it through 2 loops; 5 loops will remain on the hook; thread over and draw it through 2 loops; 4 loops will remain on the hook; thread over again and draw it through 2 loops; 3 loops will remain on the hook; thread over and draw it through 2 loops; 3 loops will remain on the hook; thread over again and draw it through 2 loop 1quintr, a quintuple treble, is now complete.

Thread over five times, put a hook beneath the 2 top threads of a next ch, and continue as before for the next quintuple tr.

2.16 Crocheting in Rows

Make a chain length (foundation chain). An extra chain may be required to make the Stitch's height, depending on the Stitch to be used. Unless otherwise noted, these chains count as the initial Stitch. Some designs call for a particular number of stitches to be "missed" at the start of the first row. This also provides the necessary height. Refer to the table below for a guide. Work a foundation row while crocheting in rows, such as trebles, then flip the work to face the reverse side after the final treble is done. Work 3 chain (turning chain) for the height, skip the preceding row's final worked Stitch, and work the following treble into the top of the next treble.

Unless the pattern specifies, always place the hook beneath the 2 top threads of each Stitch. Carry on along the row. The row's last treble will be worked onto the top of a turning chain, a 3rd chain of the previous row's starting 3ch. Some patterns require you to work into the final Stitch of the previous row instead of the turning chain at the beginning of the row if you do not work a stitch into a turning chain at the end of a row.

The following table is solely used as a reference when calculating the number of stitches necessary for a turning chain. The number of chains might vary depending on the kind and texture of thread & yarn used.

Rows of dc, dtr, htr, and other sts are worked in the same way, with the height of the turning chain variable.

2.17 Break OFF

It means to conclude or come to an end. Cut a thread to a length of 8–10cm. Pull the cut end securely through the final remaining loop on a hook. With a blunt needle, weave the end back into the main portion of the piece.

2.18 Crochet in Rounds

Unless specified in the design, never turn the work between rounds while crocheting in the rounds. Each Stitch is stitched beneath the 2 top threads of a preceding round's Stitch. In the crocheted item, there will be a "right side." A slip stitch (sl st) is used to link the rounds. Rounds may be made in several different stitches. The next example is just in the treble. Make 4ch to begin. To construct a ring, join with an sl st into a first ch. Do not distort the work in any way.

Round 1. 3 ch (for height & will count as 1 st). Work 11 trebles into the ring's center. Sl st into a 3rd ch of an initial 3ch to join the round (12tr)

Round 2. 3ch, 1tr in the same place as the sl st, 2tr in each of other tr, sl st into a 3rd ch of a starting 3ch, join the round with the sl st into a 3rd ch of the beginning 3ch (24tr)

The stitches must be uniformly increased in the following round, therefore continue as follows:

Round 3. 3ch, then * 2tr in the next tr, then 1tr in next tr; repeat from * to final st, 2tr in this st; 3ch, then Sl st into the 3rd ch of the initial 3ch to join the round (36tr). In every second Stitch, the increment was performed.

Increasing is done by combining a certain number of stitches into a single thread. The majority of patterns specify when to grow and how to do so. The goal is to keep increasing at a pace that keeps the crocheting flat.

2.19 Right vs. Left Crochet: What's the Difference?

The sole difference between the right-handed Crochet and the left-handed Crochet is the hand with which you hold the hook and the direction you stitch a row. The hook is handled in the right hand in right-handed Crochet. The right-handed maker works on stitches from right to left, with a few deviations for specialized niches of Crochet. In left-handed Crochet, the converse is true: the hook is held in the left hand, and the stitches are worked from left to right.

2.20 How to Change Colors When Crocheting?

When you're ready to change colors on a crochet project, continue the previous Stitch; however, before you, yarn over for the final time, drop the current color you're working with. Place your new color on top of the crochet hook and leave the preceding color.

Pull the new color through the previous color loops, turn the project, chain 1 (for a single chain, but if you're using double crochets or triple crochets, you'd chain two or three and). Carry on with your pattern as instructed.

Chapter 3: Crochet patterns for beginners

3.1 Knotted Headband Crochet Pattern

Materials

- Crochet hook, size; J-10 6.00 mm/ whatever hook, needed to obtain gauge.

- Lion Brand, Woolspun in the Honey/any Bulky, (5) yarn. See the chart below for the exact yardage

- Scissors

- Yarn needle

Gauge

- 12 stitches into 9 rows = 4"

- Gauge is critical for a proper fit.

Crochet Abbreviations

- sl st = slip stitch

- hdc = half double Crochet

- ch = chain

- st = stitch

Headband Size Chart & Yardage

Sizes are listed in inches for height and circumference. Yarn is in yards.

Pattern Steps

- Round 1: Ch 36 (42,48,54,60,63,66), then sl st to the first ch forming a circle, and making sure not to twist the ch.

- Round 2: Ch 1, work hdc in every st around, then sl st to a top of the first hdc, NOT the ch. 36 (42,48,54,60,63,66)

- Round 3 – 9: repeat round 2.

- Finishing: keep a 12-inch strip of the yarn hanging before fastening it off. To finish, squeeze the headband together and wrap a 12″ piece around a seam three or four times. Tie the yarn ends together and tightly weave them into the headband.

3.2 Crochet Mittens

Materials:

- Men's Version: RED HEART, "Super Saver": one skein 624, Tea Leaf A

- Child's Version; RED HEART, "Super Saver": one skein, each 387, Soft Navy B & 984 Shaded, Dusk C

- Women's Version; RED HEART, "Super Saver": one skein, each 624, Tea Leaf A & 387 Soft Navy B

- Crochet Hook: 5.5mm, [US I-9]

- Yarn needle

- Stitch markers

GAUGE: check the gauge you are using. Use any size of hook to obtain a gauge. 16 sc = 4"; 17 rows = 4".

Special Abbreviation:

Sc2tog = [insert hook in the next st, yo, draw the yarn through the st] twice, yo, draw the yarn through all of 3 loops on a hook.

Pattern Steps

The directions are for a child of 4/5 years old, While the size adjustments for "women's" and "men's" are given in the parenthesis.

The child size is 6" in diameter and 7 1/2" long. The women's size is 7 1/2" around and 11 1/2" long. The men's size is 9 1/2" around and 12" long.

Mittens:

Cuff:

Use C (B, A), and ch 15; (21, 24).

Row 1: Work in the back loops only, then sc in the 2nd ch from the hook and each ch across, then ch 1, turn.

Then repeat Row 1 for the total of 18 rows (22, 24).

Fold the cuff in half and join the ends with the slip st to form a cuff. Do not fasten it off.

Hand:

Round 1: Work along the row ends on the cuff, then slip st, evenly around for the 18 (22, 26) sts, then join the round with the slip st.

Round 2: Ch 1, place the marker, [sc in the next 8; (10, 12) sts, 2 sc in the next st] twice, Join with the slip st, [20 (24, 28) sts].

Round 3: Ch 1, [sc in the next 9 (11, 13) sts, 2 sc in the next st] twice. Join with the slip st, [22 (26, 30) sts].

Round 4: Ch 1, [sc in the next 10 (12, 14) sts, 2 sc in the next st] twice. Join with the slip st, [24 (28, 32) sts].

Child's size: Continue next step.

Women's size: Ch 1, [sc in the next 13 sts, then 2 sc in the next st] twice. Join with the slip st,(30 sts).

Men's size: Ch 1, [sc in the next 15 sts, 2 sc in the next st] twice. Join with the slip st (34 sts).

Repeat as directed, working on 1 more sc before increasing each round (38 sts).

Next Step: Continue with the stripe or solid pattern as set, for ch 1, sc in each sc around, join with the slip st. Then repeat for the total of 1 (3, 3) rounds.

Thumb Opening:

Next round: Ch 1, then [sc in a next 20 (26, 32) sts, then ch 4 (5, 6), skip the remaining sts and then join with the slip st to first st.

Upper Hand:

Sc in every st around for the 8 (10, 12) rounds; [24 (31, 38) sts], decreasing the 1 st on last round for the Women's size only [24 (30, 38) sts].

Round 1: [Sc 10 (13, 17), sc2tog] twice [22 (28, 36) sts].

Round 2: [Sc 9 (12, 16), sc2tog] twice [20 (26, 34) sts].

Round 3: [Sc 8 (11, 15), sc2tog] twice [18 (24, 32) sts].

Round 4: [Sc 7 (10, 14), sc2tog] twice [16 (22, 30) sts].

Child's size only: Sc2tog around the (8 sts), fasten off. Continue with the thumb.

Round 5: Sc in an each st around.

Round 6: [Sc 9 (13), sc2tog] twice [20 (28) sts].

Next 2 rounds: Then Sc2tog around [5 (7) sts]. Fasten it off at the end of the last round.

Thumb:

Round 1: Join the yarn to the thumb opening at the st closest to the upper hand, ch 1, sc in each st around; join with the slip st [8 (9, 12) sts]. Sc in the each st around for 4 (7, 8) rounds.

Next round: Sc2tog, then sc to 3 sts from a last st, sc last for 2 sts tog [6 (7, 10) sts]. Then Sc2tog around, working with last st as sc on a Women's size [3 (4, 5) sts]. Fasten it off. Weave in the ends.

3.3 Highland Ridge Pillow Crochet Pattern

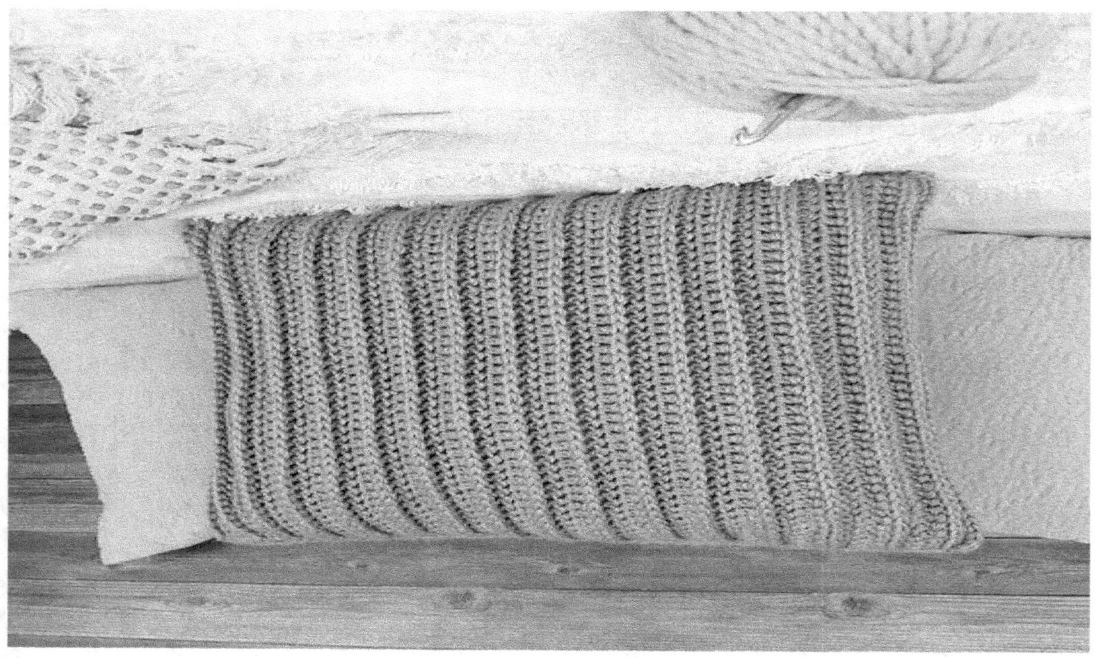

Materials

- **US Size; (6.5mm) K/10.5 crochet hook**/ size required to obtain the gauge, **18" pillow insert yarn needle, scissors,**

- Yarn: **Red Heart, Soft Essentials**, #5 bulky weight, yarn: 460 yards of #7305 Biscuit

Gauge

11 sts & 7 rows of pattern = 4"

Abbreviations

- ch(s) – chain(s),

- sc – single Crochet,

- dc – double Crochet,

- FPdc – front post double crochet,

- st(s) – stitch(es),

- sl st – slip Stitch,

- RS – right side

The Pattern

Row 1 (RS): Work on Ch 48, (1st 2 ch, count as a 1 dc) 1 dc in the 3rd ch from a hook and in each ch across; **47 dc**.

Row 2: Then Ch 2 (counts as a 1 FPdc) & turn, then 1 FPdc in an each st across; **47 FPdc**.

Row 3: Then Ch 2 (counts as a 1 dc) & turn, work on 1 dc in an each st across; **47 dc**.

Row 4-31: Repeat rows 2-3.

Row 32: Repeat row 2.

Fasten off the first piece after row 32. Then after row 32 on a second piece, do not fasten it off and then proceed to the finishing instructions.

Finishing: Hold two pieces together such that the wrong sides are in contact. On the second piece, continue with where you left off at the end of row 32: Ch 1, sc equally around three sides, passing through both pieces.

Continue down the fourth side with the pillow insert. Fasten off with an invisible link to the first sc.

3.4 Crochet Striped Sunglasses Pouch

Materials:

- Measuring tape

- **Crochet hook size** ; 5 mm / for US: H – 8 / for UK: 6.

- Needle

- **Cotton Yarn**; Color 1: <1 skein, Amount: approx. 22 g or 30 m or 33 yards, Color 2: <1 skein that is approx 22 g or 30 m or   33 yards

- **Scissors**

Gauge:

- 4 stitches & 4.5 rows per inch OR 16 stitches & 18 rows per 4 inches.

- Measured in a combination of the pattern (1 row of the hdc, 1 row of the sl st & 2 rows of an sc st).

- 1.5 stitches & 1.8 rows per cm OR 16 stitches & 18 rows per 10 cm.

Size & Measurements:

- Length: 16 cm or 6.25 inches

- Width: 9 cm or 3.5 inches

Abbreviations:

- CB = color B

- CA = color A

- Ch = chain (s)

- Prev = previous

- Hdc = half double crochet

- Sc = single crochet

- St = stitch (es)

- Sl st = slip stitch

The Pattern:

With CA work on ch 15 st.

- Row 1 with the CA: Ch 1 (counts as the 1st st), work sc 1 in all the ch from prev row, then turn (14 st).

- Row 2 with the CB: Ch 2 st, (counts as the 1st st), work hdc 1 in all the st from prev row, the turn (14 st).

- Row 3 with the CB: Ch 1 (counts as the 1st st), work sl st 1 through the back look in all the st from a prev row, then turn (14 st).

- Row 4-5 with the CA: Ch 1 (counts as the 1st st); work sc 1 in all the st from the prev row, then turn (14 st).

- Row 6-25: Repeat row 2-5; 5 times, with the respective colors.

- Row 26 with the CB: Repeat row 2.

- Row 27 with the CB: Repeat row 3.

- Row 28 with the CA: Repeat row 4-5; once.

- Row 29 with the CA: Ch 1 (counts as the 1st st); work sc 1 through the back, then look all st from the prev row, turn (14 st)

- Row 30-53: Repeat row 2-5; 6 times, with the respective colors.

- Row 54 with the CB: Repeat row 2.

- Row 55 with the CB: Repeat row 3.

- Row 56 with the CA: Repeat row 4-5; once.

- Fasten off and cut yarn.

Finishing:

• Tighten the threads and weave in the ends.

• Sew side seams or crochet the pouch together with the slip stitches after folding it twice.

3.5 Crochet Baby Booties

Materials

- 3.0-mm Hook (D/3 USA, 11 UK)

- 3.5-mm Hook (E/4 USA, 9 UK)

- Tapestry Needle

- Sport Weight Yarn or DROPS Baby Merino in two different colors (4 PLY)

Yardage

You'll just need a small amount of yarn. For this pattern, 22 g of yarn is used for the 0–3-month booties & 26 g for 3–6-month baby booties.

Crochet Abbreviations (Us Terms)

- BPdc – Back Post Double Crochet

- BLO – Back Loop Only

- Ch – Chain

- BPdc2tog – Back Post, Double Crochet, Two Together

- Dc – Double Crochet

- FPdc2tog; Front Post Double Crochet, Two Together

- FPdc – Front Post Double Crochet

- Sl St – Slip Stitch

- Inc – Increase

- Sc – Single Crochet

- Hdc; Half Double Crochet

- Yo – Yarn Over

- St – Stitch

Size: 0-3 Months

Length; 9 cm (3.5")

Gauge

For Gauge check that your sole measures: 3.5" (9 cm)

Pattern Steps

Bootie Sole

Use white yarn and hook of 3.0-mm (D), ch 13.

1. Create 2 dc in the third loop from a hook. Then make 8 dc: [7 dc] all in the last loop. Work on other loops of starting chain then makes 8 dc. Then Crochet [3 dc], all in the first loop. Link with the sl st into the top loop of 2-ch spacing. (28 sts)

2. Work on Ch 2, 1 dc in same st, where you joined the previous round. Work 2 dc inc, then 8 dc, then 7 dc inc, then 8 dc, then 3 dc inc. Link by the sl st for the previous round. (42 sts)

3. Ch 1, do sc in same st, then 1 sc inc; (1 sc, 1 sc inc) twice, then 3 sc, then 2 hdc, then 3 dc. (1 dc inc, 1 dc) 3 times. Do 2 dc inc, (1 dc, 1 dc inc) 3 times, then 3 dc, then 2 hdc, then 3 sc, (1 sc inc, 1 sc) 3 times. Link by the sl st into the first ch. (56 sts)

4. Ch 1, do sl st in back loops; only all around. (56 sts)

Body Of the Bootie

Join contrasting colors.

5. Ch 2, work on 1 dc in BLO all around; (56 sts)

6. Ch 1; work (4 FPdc, 4 BPdc) for the 7 times. Link by sl st into first st; (56 sts)

7. Ch 1, work (do FPdc, FPdc2tog, FPdc, then BPdc, BPdc2tog, again BPdc); for the 7 times. Link by the sl st into the first st. (42 sts)

8. Work Ch 1, work (BPdc, then BPdc2tog, FPdc, then FPdc2tog); for the 7 times. Link by the sl st into the first st; (28 sts)

9. Work Ch 1 (2 BPdc and 2 FPdc); for the three times. BPdc2tog, then FPdc2tog. (2 BPdc and 2 FPdc); for the 3 times. Link by the sl st into first st; (26 sts).

10. Work Ch 1, (2 BPdc and 2 FPdc); twice. Work 2 FPdc. Then BPdc2tog, FP/BPdc2tog, FPdc2tog. (2 BPdc, 2 FPdc); do it twice. Then 2 BPdc. Link

by the sl st into first st; (23 sts)

Ankle

Switch to a 3.5-mm (E) size hook so that the bootie will be a bit softer around the ankle and leg.

11. Ch 2, work dc in each st around;

link by sl st; (23 sts).

12. Ch 2, work dc in each st around, with one increase, at the end (create 2 dc in last st), joined by the sl st. (24 sts)

Turn your work around so you're crocheting in the opposite direction of what you've been doing. If not, flip the bootie inside out and keep crocheting in the same manner.

13. Ch 1, (3 FPdc, 3 BPdc); all around. Link by sl st; (24 sts).

14. Repeat the round 13; (24 sts). The white yarn is attached again.

15. Ch 1, work sc in each st; all around, link by sl st; (24 sts). Fasten off the ends.

3.6 Crochet Mug Hug and Rug

Materials

- Crochet hook; 4mm hook or in a suitable size.

- Cotton yarn/ any other yarn that does not feel when washed.

- Large darning needle; for sewing.

- Two buttons.

- Pair of scissors.

- Threading needle.

- Sewing thread; to attach buttons.

Gauge

4 STS = 1"

Size

Fits standard 10 oz coffee mugs.

Pattern Steps

Crochet the Mug Rug

Begin by making a slip knot on your hook. Chain No. 16 Little bumps may be seen on the rear of your chain, whereas 'v' shapes can be seen on the front of the chain. Our initial row will be crocheted into the bumps on the backside. Crochet 15 single crochets until the chain is complete. Chain 1 and turn your work when you approach the end of the row. The additional chain aids in turning and neatening the edges.

Continue working 15sc rows, chaining 1 it after every row, unless you have 15 rows. Using your darning needle, cut the yarn and stitch in the ends. Don't worry if the square is a little crooked; the next edging will help straighten it up. Crochet the mug rug's border with a different color yarn now. Begin by making a slip knot on the hook and doing single Crochet on one of the square's sides. Chain 1, skip a stitch, single Crochet.

Make a single crochet in the corner, chain 1, then create another single crochet in the same Stitch. Then make your next single Crochet by chaining 1, skipping a stitch. Slip Stitch into the first single crochet of the round to complete the circle. Make another round in the same manner with a different color, but this time work the single crochets into chain 1 spaces from the previous round. The seed stitch is the name for this technique. Continue with the seed stitch for two more rows, concluding with the final row in the same colors as your mug rug's centerpiece.

Crochet the Mug Hug

Chain 31 starts with a slip knot on the hook. Make 28 double crochets in the bumps on the back of the chain (extra three chains for turning).

Turn your work after chaining three times. In the same Stitch as that of chain 3, work the next double Crochet. Double Crochet till the end of the row, then increase by creating two double crochets in the same Stitch in the last Stitch. Continue in this manner until you've completed 5 rows of dcs with an increase at the beginning and end of each row. Work the double Crochet through each Stitch until you approach the end, without increasing. In the final Stitch, do not increase. There are now six rows.

Finish off our work with a single crochet border. This is the corner; work 3 single crochets across the double Crochet that is currently on. Continue working 2 single crochets over each double Crochet till you reach the next corner. Make three single crochet stitches. Now that you've reached the original beginning chain, Single Crochet into the 'V' forms until you've reached the end. To make the button loop, work 2 single crochets around the next double crochet and chain 20. To finish the corner, work another single crochet in the same space. In each of the following two double crochets, add two more single crochets. Chain 17 to make a second button loop when you reach the final row. Finish your border by crocheting 3 single crochets in the corner & 1 single crochet in each stitch after that. Pull up a loop between the first and second double Crochet of a top row with a different yarn color. Pull up a loop &

pull through the loop on your hook with your hook in between the next two stitches. Continue slipping stitching around the next Stitch until you come to the end of the row.

Using the slip stitch, make two additional stripes. Sew on the buttons using your two buttons, sewing thread, and threading needle. Make sure they're in the corners of your work. Now is the moment to stitch in any remaining ends. Sew the ends in with your darning needle. It's typically a good idea to introduce the ends of your work to the rear and stitch them in there so they're hidden from view.

3.7 Easy Crochet Basket

Materials

- **crochet hook, size H** (5.00mm) / size needed to have a gauge

- Approximately 200 yards of bulky/ 315 yards of super bulky yarn

- Tapestry needle & scissors

- **Stitch marker**

Size & Gauge:

Rounds 1-9= 4"; diameter circle (bulky) / 5.5" diameter circle; (super bulky),

Finished basket measures approximately 10" wide & 6" high (bulky) / 11.5" wide & 8" high (super bulky)

Pattern Steps:

- With Color A, create a magic loop.

- Round 1: ch 1, work sc 6 into the magic loop, and pull it tight. (6)

- Round 2: work directly into first st of previous round, work 2sc in each st around; (12)

- Round 3: work *2sc in the first st, work sc in the next st, then repeat from * around. (18)

- Round 4: work *2sc in the first st, work sc 2, repeat the * around. (24)

- Round 5: work *2sc in the first st, work sc 3, repeat from the * around. (30)

- Round 6: work *2sc in the first st, work sc 4, repeat the * around. (36)

- Round 7: Work *2sc in the first st, work sc 5, repeat from the* around. (42)

- Round 8: Work *2sc in the first st, work sc 6, repeat from the * around. (48)

- Round 9: Work *2sc in the first st, work sc 7, repeat the * around. (54)

- Round 10: Work*2sc in the first st, work sc 8, repeat from the * around. (60)

- {note that pattern repeats, change up at this point to ensure the bottom of basket can be placed flat}

- Round 11: Work *sc 5, work 2sc in the next st, work sc 4, repeat from the * around. (66)

- Round 12: Work *sc 3, work 2sc in the next st, work sc 7, repeat from the * around. (72)

- Round 13: Work *sc 9, work 2sc in the next st, work sc 2, repeat from the * around. (78)

- Round 14: Work *2sc in the first st, work sc 12, repeat from the * around. (84)

- Round 15: work *sc 7, work 2sc in the next st, work sc 6, repeat from the * around. (90)

- Round 16: work *sc 3, 2sc in the next st, work sc 11, repeat from the * around. (96)

- Round 17: Work *sc 11, work 2sc in the next st, sc 4, repeat it from the * around. (102)

- Round 18: Work *sc 6, work 2sc in the next st, work sc 10, repeat from the * around. (108)

- Slip Stitch into first st, of round 18, turn your work (the wrong side is facing you).

- Round 19: work ch 1& sl st into each stitch around. (108)

- Turn work so that the right side is facing you.

- Round 20: work ch 1, sc into each sl st around, work sl st to the top of the first sc. (108)

- Round 21: Work ch 1, work sc into the same st as join & in each st around, work sl st to the top of first st; (108), then

- *switch to Color B

- Round 22-32: Work ch 1, sc into the same st, as join & in each st around, work sl st to the top of the first st. (108); then *switch to Color C

- Round 33-41: work ch 1, work sc into the same st, as join & in each st around, work sl st to the top of the first st. (108)

- Round 42: work ch 1, sc 23, then on ch 12, sk next 8 sc, then sc 46, then to ch 12, sk next 8 sc, work sc 23, work sl st to the top of the first st. (116)

- Round 43: Work ch 1, sc 22, work sc in the next st, one row below, work hdc 16 in the chain space, work sc in the next st, one row below, work sc 44, sc in the next st, one row below, work hdc 16 in the chain space, work sc in the next st, one row below, work sc 22, use the invisible join to the end. (124). Then Fasten off & weave in the ends.

Chapter 4: Common Crochet Mistakes and How to Solve Them?

Nobody is exempt from making the same mistakes, whether they are just learning to crochet or have years of expertise. It's quite OK to make these common crochet mistakes! It is preferable to be aware of such time-suckers in order to avoid problems that might derail your efforts.

Here are a few typical crochet mistakes and some pointers on how to fix or prevent doing them in the future.

4.1 Crochet is not the same as crochet.

The term "crochet" has been used by crocheters to describe their craft. Crochet is completed with a single hook, while crochet is completed with two needles. Crochet hooks are often referred to as crochet needles; however, while crocheting, you will need one.

4.2 Failing to make a gauge swatch.

The gauge of a crochet fabric measuring 4 by 4 inches is the number of stitches and rows in the cloth. The designer has included a gauge to confirm that the project is of the proper size before starting work on it. It will be frustrating to put in many hours into a project only to learn that it is either too little or much too huge when it is completed.

Assume that your pattern calls for a medium-weight yarn and an I/9-sized crochet hook. In 4 inches of material, there are 8 rows of single crochet stitches and 12 single crochet stitches across the 4 inches. Check the figures (if any are provided) against the pattern's gauge. If they're somewhat close to one other or match, you're fine to go. If this is not the case, you will need to increase the tension or switch to different hook size. Granted, a gauge is not required for all crafts, but it is essential if you are manufacturing apparel.

4.3 Crocheting only in the front loop

If you're just starting out with crochet, it's easy to make this mistake. Getting the hang of where to position the hook in each Stitch is the basis of the craft. If you make this mistake, it might be because you didn't properly understand how to crochet, or it could be because your hook slips every now and then, and you aren't experienced enough to identify the mistake right away. Spending extra time reviewing each row that you work is an excellent method for avoiding this blunder in the future. Even though it may seem tedious at first, now that you've mastered the fundamental concept of crocheting both under loops, you should practice double-checking your stitches until they're second nature.

4.4 Your Project Keeps Getting Wider

This is a typical gaffe that almost everyone does at some time in their lives. When you first begin a project, you may assume it to be really straightforward, believing that it is just a matter of repeating the same Stitch over and over again. After an hour, you see that your rectangle blanket has been transformed into a hexagonal shape.

This difficulty occurs when you do not count your stitches correctly and wind up working more stitches than are required to complete the project. It's possible that you're doubling up into one stitch or that you're working a stitch within the turning chain by mistake. The most effective approach to prevent making this mistake is to keep track of your stitches! Choose between counting each row as you finish it or paying close attention to the overall shape of your work. Don't waste time working quickly just to realize that you forgot to add Stitch 10 rows back.

4.5 You Aren't Checking Your Rows While Working

Keeping your time as useful as possible is the focus of this point, as well as the one that came before. When crocheting, the rows must be counted in the same manner as the stitches must be counted throughout the crocheting process. The most straightforward solution to this problem is to use a row counter. That may be anything as sophisticated as a computerized row counter that counts each row with a single click, or it could be something as simple as a pen and notepad and making a small tick after each finished row.

4.6 Confusing U.S. And U.K. Crochet Terms

Because there are so many designs available on the internet, you may come across some that are labeled in British English. If you're from the United Kingdom, that's excellent, but if you're from the United States, you should be aware that the terminology varies from the United States to the United Kingdom. In the United States, single crochet is the same as double crochet, which is the same as triple crochet in the United Kingdom.

When it comes to working patterns, you will observe how that might make a difference. Use this table to convert terminology from the United Kingdom to the United States.

4.7 Using a different yarn weight and expecting the same result as the pattern

When it comes to successfully following a crochet pattern, the weight of the yarn is really crucial. The gauge of your finished item will change if you attempt to construct a thick scarf from a design that asks for #6 yarn, but you only have #5.

Almost every design is developed with a certain yarn in mind, and even a tiny weight variation may have a tremendous impact on the outcome. If you are using up all of the yarn you have on hand, it is advised that you complete your gauge swatch. This can help you determine what alterations you'll need to make to the design in order to get it as close as feasible.

4.8 Using an Incorrect Hook Size

This, as well as the prior two recommendations, are both typical errors to make. Making the mistake of using the wrong hook size may have a huge influence on the outcome of your project. Each pattern is written with a certain hook size in mind, and modifying it will result in stitches that are either too tight or too loose as a consequence of the adjustment.

Make sure you carefully study the pattern to verify that you're using the correct size needle for the project. Make sure to include your gauge swatch in your project as well. However, if your gauge swatch turns out to be erroneous and you discover it before you begin, you will have saved yourself a great deal of time from having to re-do the whole job!

4.9 Not reading the entire crochet pattern before starting

When starting a new project, the essential thing to remember to do is to look through each and every line carefully. All that is left for you to do now is grab your yarn and crochet hook and get starting! Following your first encounter with crochet designs, you will realize that not reading the pattern first is a common error. However, it is possible that it will not make a major impact in every instance.

Preparing for the pattern by reading it beforehand will allow you to get familiar with a new stitch before starting. Despite the fact that you do not have to recall each step, reading through a pattern is comparable to studying for an exam before actually taking it. To begin a new crochet project as soon as possible is always the best option.

4.10 Incorrectly counting the starting chain/not knowing where to place the first Stitch

The first chain of each crochet creation serves as the foundation (possibly one of the least pleasurable aspects). One of the first jobs you'll learn to do while learning to crochet is chaining. It's also one of the most challenging.

It is one of the most common blunders that people make while chaining because they do not place their beginning stitch in the right chain. This will result in either an excessive number of or an insufficient number of stitches, and if you aren't keeping track of them, your project will be doomed from the start. The most straightforward strategy to preventing or solving this problem is to get intimately acquainted with the concepts of chaining and counting chains.

4.11 Failure to Leave a Long Enough Yarn Tail

The process of weaving in the ends is perhaps the part of crocheting that everyone dislikes the most. Not only can you not cut the yarn and hope no one sees it, but you will also have difficulty later on due to the fact that your strand is too short.

There's no difference between adding a new ball of yarn, tying off a project, or switching between various colors of yarn; you always need to leave enough length to weave in the ends properly. To make this method as simple as possible, it is advised that you leave at least 5-6 inches of yarn on the loom.

4.12 Crocheting too loosely or too firmly or altering the tension.

It's critical to maintain a continuous level of tension throughout the performance. One approach for doing this is to take your time. It is more vital to concentrate on sewing nice, even stitches than it is to focus on speed; speed will follow eventually. If you crochet them too tightly, you'll have problems working the subsequent row since you'll be trying to get the hook into the stitches as you go. The incorrect gauge will result from crocheting too loosely, as will a messy appearance to the finished item. If your tension changes much, your finished product will be uneven and crooked.

4.13 Your project's sides grow or shrink.

This is a relatively frequent mistake made by newcomers. Knowing where to work the first stitch of each row, the final Stitch, and how many chain stitches to do at the beginning of each row are the keys to having good even edges.

The following are the rules for starting each row:

• 1 chain stitch in single Crochet

• 2 chain stitches in half double Crochet

• 3 chain stitches in double Crochet

• 5 chain stitches in treble or triple Crochet

Put the last Stitch into the preceding row's top chain stitch. Make it a habit to count your stitches throughout a row as well. You'll always end up with attractive even sides if you start and stop at the precise locations and count stitches.

This list will be useful in your crochet journey. Always keep in mind that you are not alone in making crochet errors and that you will be able to look back and grin at how far you have gone over time!

Abbreviations Used

Reading crochet designs is just like reading a foreign language with a lot of acronyms. It may be difficult at first, but shorthand will quickly become second nature. It's a good idea to familiarize yourself with the crochet stitch dictionary, but here's a quick rundown of acronyms that novices are likely to encounter:

- **ch** = chain stitch
- **beg** = beginning
- **dec** = decrease
- **ch-sp** = chain space
- **inc** = increase
- **dc** = double Crochet
- **mc** = main color
- **rs** = right side
- **rep** = repeat
- **sl st** = slip Stitch
- **sc** = single Crochet
- **tr** = treble Crochet
- **st** = stitch

- **ws** = wrong side

- YO =Yarn over

Conclusion

Crochet for beginners is a book that teaches you how to knit if you've had no experience with the craft previously. Learn all you need to know about the tools and supplies you'll need, as well as how to properly use them, in this course. The language of crochet and pattern design might be tough to grasp at times, but this book has made it easier for you to comprehend so that you can pick it up and start crocheting right away. When learning to crochet, basic stitches are vital, and you can learn all you need to know about them right here. You have complete freedom to practise as much as you want and at your own pace.

Once you've learned these stitches, you may go on to more sophisticated techniques and stitch learning opportunities. Left-handers and right-handers may equally benefit from this advice. Your crochet talents will increase as you go, and you'll be able to vary your movements as you use your crochet hook to develop a rhythm as you go along. Working with yarns might be difficult at first, but once you get the hang of it, it will become second nature. This book contains some useful crochet ideas and strategies that will help you complete your project more quickly and efficiently. Making errors is difficult because you have to learn from them in order to go forward. However, the most typical crochet missteps, as well as the best tactics for avoiding them, are discussed in detail. After you've gotten started and feel confident enough to try out some patterns, you may go on to more complex designs that include a variety of stitches taught in this book. It is possible to go one step further and experiment with more elaborate designs whenever you are ready. There are a few of intermediate and advanced patterns that involve stitches that you'll become accustomed to working with. So best of luck to you! Crochet novels have soared in popularity in recent years. Many different authors contribute to them, and they cover an array of themes. They all have something unique to offer as a prize. Thank you for adding this book on your reading list, despite the fact that there are so many more to choose from.